The Star Still Beckons

GIFTS OF PRESENCE AT ADVENT AND CHRISTMASTIDE

LEONARD SWEET

The Salish
Sea Press
Orcas Island
Washington

Copyright © 2025 by Leonard Sweet

All rights reserved.

No part of this book may be reproduced in any form or by any electronic or mechanical means, including information storage and retrieval systems, without written permission from the author, except for the use of brief quotations in a book review.

ISBN hardcover: 978-1-63613-039-2

ISBN paperback: 978-1-63613-043-9

ISBN ebook: 978-1-63613-040-8

Published by The Salish Sea Press. Box 1492, Absecon, NJ 08201.

The Salish Sea Press is a program of SpiritVenture Ministries.

leonardsweet.com

Cover, interior design and illustrations by Kris White

"God has Favored" donkey image by Kim Guthrie, Used by permission. kimguthrieart.com

Scripture quotations taken from The Holy Bible, New International Version®, NIV®. Copyright © 1973, 1978, 1984, 2011 by Biblica, Inc. Used with permission of Zondervan. All rights reserved worldwide. www.zondervan.com

The Holy Bible, English Standard Version® (ESV®) © 2001 by Crossway, a publishing ministry of Good News Publishers. All rights reserved.

Contents

Dedication Meditation: The Humble Bearer	ix
Introduction	xv
Week One *From Glory to Grime*	1
Week Two *The Manger Manifesto*	11
Week Three *The Sacred Dance of Silence and Song*	23
Week Four *The First Christmas Carol*	33
Christmas Eve *O Holy Night*	41
Christmas Day *The Enchantment of Wonder*	49
Hogmanay—New Year Beginning *When The Saints Go Hobbling In—Living as Both Answer and Mystery*	59
Interactives *Prayerful Ponderings and Sacred Reflections*	71
Notes	85
About the Author	87

"God Has Favored" by Kim Guthrie, Used by permission.

Dedication

To Issy the donkey*
and donkeys everywhere,
(the symbol of the tribe of Issachar)

*See St. Is (2020), St. As (2021), and St. Us (forthcoming 2026), the Jesus story as told by Mary's donkey Issy, by Lisa Samson and Leonard Sweet.

THE HUMBLE BEARER: DEDICATION MEDITATION

> The ox knows its owner, and the donkey its master's crib; but Israel does not know, my people do not understand.
>
> —ISAIAH 1:3 ESV

Beyond the familiar faces in nativity scenes lies a curious pattern, one that makes us wonder if animals grasp divine mysteries more naturally than we do. While poring over centuries of Christmas art for this devotional, I noticed something striking: in paintings, tapestries, and carvings, it's often the stable creatures who seem most attuned to the holy moment unfolding before them.

The oxen bow their heads in reverence. The sheep gather close, as if drawn by an unseen force. And most touchingly, there's an ancient Christian artistic tradition, noted by scholar Laura Hobgood-Oster, of carving scenes where a donkey bends to tenderly "kiss" the infant Jesus.[1] While this particular image still eludes me, its symbolism haunts: could it be that our animal companions, unburdened by human cares and complexity, sometimes perceive sacred truths more clearly than we do?

Sometimes the most profound truths come wrapped in the most plain, even plaintive packages. Consider the donkey—that steady, sturdy creature that threads its way through the greatest story ever told—not as a mere beast of burden but as a bearer of holy mysteries.

In the ancient world, kings rode horses to war but donkeys in times of peace. A horse spoke of power and might; a donkey whispered of humility and wisdom. While horses could be driven to exhaustion by their riders' ambitions, donkeys knew their limits. While horses might plunge ahead into dangerous waters, donkeys would pause, assess, then choose the safer path. The Greeks saw donkeys as symbols of the lower classes. The Hebrews saw them as creatures in need of redemption. Yet it was this humble animal that God chose as companion and carrier through the pivotal moments of salvation history.

You can't tell the Christmas story without featuring the donkey. The first Christmas journey involves a young woman, heavy with divine promise, making her way to Bethlehem. Beneath her, the donkey picks its path carefully through the Judean hills, bearing not just Mary, but the very Word made Flesh. Those enormous ears—the ones that can swivel at the slightest sound—perhaps caught the first whispered prayers of the mother-to-be. Maybe they heard Mary singing what we now know as the Magnificat, that ancient song of praise echoing the same themes as Psalm 22, which Jesus would later sing from the cross. And those donkey eyes—penetrating yet patient, able to spot danger long before humans notice—kept faithful watch through the cold nights.

In the stable, the donkey stood vigil. The prophet Isaiah had written "The ox knows its owner, and the donkey its master's crib" (Isaiah 1:3). Here was a donkey, witnessing the birth of the Master of all creation and maybe even bending down to breathe his warm breath on the baby's crib to keep it warm. The Greek word for "manger" is phatne–the same word used for a donkey's feedbox. The lowest of animals offered its dinner table to become the first throne of the King of Kings.

Later, when Herod's fury threatened the holy child, it was a donkey that carried the holy family to safety in Egypt. The same creature that had once spoken to save Balaam from destruction, now bore in silence the Savior of the world. The same beast that had carried Abraham's wood of sacrifice, now carried the One who would become the final sacrifice.

Years later, on what we now call Palm Sunday, Jesus chose not a majestic stallion but a young donkey for his triumphal entry into Jerusalem. The King of Peace rode on the beast of peace, fulfilling Zechariah's ancient prophecy (Zechariah 9:9). The cross-shaped marking on the donkey's back—a marking that tradition says came from the shadow of Calvary—bore the weight of the One who would soon bear the cross.

The donkey's tale whispers to us still: sometimes the holiest path is the humblest one.

In our rush to reach the manger this Advent, perhaps we should take a lesson from the donkey's pace. This is an animal that cannot be hurried, that chooses its steps with care, that knows the difference between what its master asks, what the task requires, and what the crowd demands. The donkey reminds us that God's greatest works often come disguised in humility and the unadorned, that wisdom sometimes looks like stubbornness, and that the most important journey is not always the fastest one.

As we prepare our hearts for Christmas, let us remember the quiet dignity of the creature that bore Christ into our world. Let us learn from its patient strength, its humble service, its deep wisdom. For if God could work through such an unexpected messenger, imagine what divine purposes might be worked through us.

The donkey's tale whispers to us still: Sometimes the holiest path is the humblest one. Sometimes the greatest wisdom lies in knowing our limits. And sometimes—perhaps most times—God's greatest gifts come to those who, like Mary's gentle mount, are content to bear Christ into the world without fanfare or glory, one gawky, awkward, but sure-footed step at a time.

A PRAYER FOR ADVENT

> Divine Bearer of our burdens
> Who chose the lowly donkey as your throne,
> Grant us the wisdom to walk slowly in these sacred days,
>
> To know our limits as clearly
> as your humble servant beast,

To bear your presence as faithfully as that first
Christmas companion.

When we would rush headlong into waters too deep,
Teach us the donkey's discernment.

When we would bow to the world's demands for speed,
Grant us the donkey's steady pace.

When we would seek glory in great things,
Remind us of the holiness of humble service.

Make us, like Mary's gentle mount,
Bearers of the sacred presence,
Sure-footed in faith's journey,
Unafraid of narrow paths that lead to Bethlehem.

Make us, like Balaam's wise beast,
Attuned to angels in our path,
Brave enough to halt before danger,
True to heaven's voice when earth's wisdom fails.

Make us, like Palm Sunday's faithful servant,
Humble carriers of hope's triumph,
Willing to bear both praise and scorn,
Knowing we serve a kingdom not of this world.

May we bear your light into the dark places,
Your hope into the hard places,
Your love into the lonely places,
One careful step at a time.
Amen.

Introduction

SOMEWHERE IN THE STORY

In *The Hope of Glory*, Pulitzer Prize-winning historian Jon Meacham reflects on Jesus' last words from the cross. Meacham, an Episcopalian and former church vestry member, shares a remarkable story in his chapter on "Father, forgive them, for they know not what they do."

The story concerns Richmond Lattimore, the renowned classical scholar and translator of Greek texts, including the New Testament. Though Lattimore regularly attended mass with his wife at the Episcopal Church of the Good Shepherd in

INTRODUCTION

Rosemont, he never received Holy Communion. His friend, Father Andrew Mead, had always assumed Lattimore was a skeptic. Yet late in life, Lattimore made the surprising decision to be baptized.

> "Dr. Lattimore," Andrew asked, "I thought you had reservations about the Christian faith and the church."
> "I did," Lattimore replied.
> "But you don't any longer?"
> "No, not any longer."
> "Please, then, may I ask you, when did they go away?"
> "Somewhere in Saint Luke."[1]

Those four words—"Somewhere in Saint Luke"—capture something profound about faith's gentle unfolding. Each of us has our own story of when doubt began to give way to faith, when questions quarried quests. For some, that moment came while reading Paul's letters to the Romans or the Colossians. For others, it was in the ancient poetry of the Psalms. For me, it was the Gospel of John. And for many, like Lattimore, it was somewhere in Luke's careful account of Jesus' life.

The Christmas story, woven through Luke's gospel, has often been that sacred space where skepticism softens and faith takes root. Somewhere in the journey to Bethlehem, somewhere in the wonder of shepherds, somewhere in the songs of angels—that's where many of us first glimpsed the divine narrative into which we were being invited.

This devotional seeks to create such sacred spaces—moments where doubt might give way to wonder, where questions might blossom into revelation. From a humble manger to the cosmic dance of the Trinity, from shepherds' whispers to angels' proclamations, from silent nights to joyous carols—we'll explore the Christmas story as a living invitation into divine presence.

INTRODUCTION

Each week unfolds a distinct facet of this transfiguring narrative. We begin with "From Glory to Grime," discovering how the Author of Life chose to write divinity into humanity's messiest chapters. Here, we encounter a God who doesn't merely touch our story but fully immerses in it—from a cradle in a cesspit to a cross on a garbage dump.

In "The Manger Manifesto," we explore how the Incarnation declares that all matter matters, upending our understanding of worth and dignity. This divine "I CARE" echoes through the cosmos, challenging our world's antimatter messages with the revolutionary truth of Emmanuel.

"The Sacred Dance of Silence and Song" invites us to experience both the contemplative hush of "Silent Night" Christianity and the exuberant joy of "Jingle Bells" faith. Here, we discover how silence flows from the outside in, while stillness radiates from the inside out.

In "The First Christmas Carol," we delve into the power of prepositions over propositions, finding in Emmanuel—God WITH us—the first and greatest carol ever sung. This divine witness becomes not just a theological concept but a lived reality, inviting us into the eternal dance of the Trinity.

The journey moves through Christmas Eve's "O Holy Night" and Christmas Day's "Enchantment of Wonder," before carrying us into the New Year with a Hogmanay reflection on "When The Saints Go Hobbling In." Here, as we cross the threshold into a new beginning, we discover ourselves as both answers to prayer and stewards of sacred mysteries—learning to hobble our way to glory just as the saints before us did.

Throughout these pages, you'll find not just devotional readings but invitations to engage—through "Prayerful Ponderings and Sacred Reflections" that encourage deeper exploration of each theme. These interactive elements convert private reading into communal discovery and personal reflection into shared wisdom.

INTRODUCTION

Like Lattimore, we might find our own faith awakening "somewhere in Saint Luke." Or perhaps it will be somewhere in these pages, as we explore the depths of divine love made manifest in Bethlehem. For the Word who became Flesh still dwells among us, transfiguring our moments of grime into glimpses of glory, our silence into song, our matter into meaning.

The star that guided wise men still beckons, calling us to find in Christmas not just a historical event but an ongoing encounter with Love Incarnate. As we journey through Advent and Christmastide together, may we each discover our own "somewhere"—that sacred space where heaven touches earth, where doubt gives way to discovery, where enlightenment gives way to wonderment, where parchment gives way to sacrament, and where we find ourselves drawn ever deeper into the greatest story ever told.

The star still beckons. Shall we follow?

🎵 *Special Note:* Let me encourage you—speak the Advent prayers aloud if possible. Release them. Speak them into the air where words become more than ink—they become atmosphere. If a phrase resonates with you, say it over a few times, linger, and let it echo then settle down into your being. Let your breath prayers become Bethlehem's breeze.

INTRODUCTORY ADVENT PRAYER

Gracious God, you meet us all somewhere along the way—in ancient texts and timeless truths, in moments of questioning and seasons of certainty.

We give thanks for your patient presence as our faith unfolds, page by page, chapter by chapter, story by story.

Just as you drew Richmond Lattimore to yourself through Luke's careful words, you continue to invite each of us deeper into your divine narrative.

In this Advent season, help us remember how you entered our story in Bethlehem and how you enter our lives anew each day.

Whether we find you in Luke's nativity, in Paul's letters, in David's psalms, or in countless other sacred passages, guide us as we journey from doubt to devotion, from reservation to revelation.

Grant us the wisdom to recognize those holy moments when our concerns give way to convictions and our questions give way to quests, and the grace to welcome others who are still searching for their "somewhere" in your Story.

As we prepare our hearts for Christmas, may we remain open to encountering you in unexpected places and unforeseen ways. Through Christ our Lord, who beckons us all into his story of love and healing. Amen.

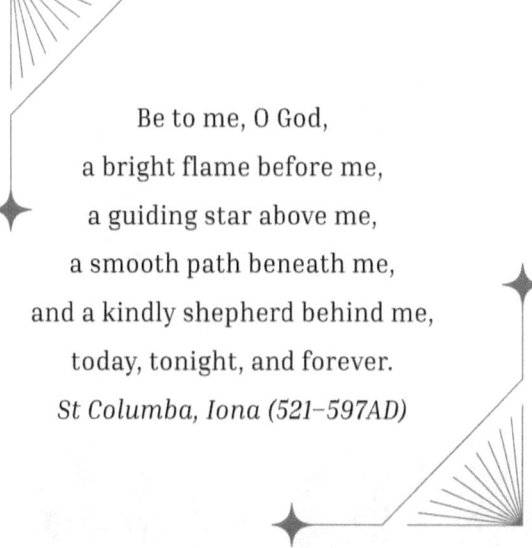

Be to me, O God,
a bright flame before me,
a guiding star above me,
a smooth path beneath me,
and a kindly shepherd behind me,
today, tonight, and forever.
St Columba, Iona (521–597AD)

Week One

FROM GLORY TO GRIME

IN THE BEGINNING was the Story, and the Story was with God, and the Story was God. Every great story that has ever been told echoes this original Story—the divine narrative that shaped creation itself. And then, in an act of unimaginable creativity, the Story became Flesh and dwelt among us. The Author stepped into the Author's own narrative, not merely to tell us about divine love, but to live it among us, page by page, breath by breath. And then, as all great stories must, this Story conquered death itself, bursting forth from the tomb on the third day to write new life into every page of creation.

Emmanuel: God WITH Us

The power is in the Prepositions. Not the Propositions. Prepositions are relational words. For example, "Christ IN you" or "In Christ," which is used almost 200 times in the Second Testament. The Incarnation is the ultimate act of *withness*—God stepping into human existence to dwell with us, share our joys and sufferings, and bridge the divine and the human. It is a profound manifestation of divine solidarity and presence. "God with us" becomes not just a theological statement but a lived reality, inviting humanity into a deeper relationship rooted in love, accompaniment, and shared life. I used to be a piano accompanist for musicians. The Holy Spirit is God's ultimate accompanist, fingers dancing across the keys of our lives with perfect pitch and timing. Just as I once sat at the piano bench, eyes fixed not on my own hands but on the musician I served, the Spirit keeps divine time with the melody of Christ that wants to emerge from the symphony of our days.

The Spirit doesn't perform solos or steal the spotlight—this is backup ministry at its most sublime. Every grace note, every harmonic enhancement, every perfectly timed entrance serves one purpose: to make the music of Jesus sound richer, fuller, and more beautiful through the instrument of our lives. The Spirit reads our tempo when we rush ahead in anxiety, slows us down when we drag behind in doubt, and bridges the awkward pauses when we lose our place in the score.

This is accompaniment as holy calling—not following our lead, but helping us follow Jesus. The Spirit turns our fumbling attempts at discipleship into something that actually sounds like Jesus to a world desperate for that particular song. Every day becomes a duet with the divine, where two sets of hands—ours and the Spirit's—create music that neither could make alone.

The question isn't whether we can carry the tune, but whether we're willing to let the Spirit set the rhythm and fill in the harmony that makes our small part of the larger composition sing. "Withness" means salvation is not achieved from afar but through the intimate, incarnate presence of God in the person of Jesus Christ.[1] A preposition is more powerful than a proposition because while a proposition explains something about life, a preposition enters into it. A proposition says, "Here's the truth," but a preposition says, "Here I am—with you." After all, withness is the heart of the Incarnation, and no proposition ever changed the world the way "God with us" did.

The relational nuance of prepositions transforms abstract theological truths into vivid, relational expressions. In this way, even the smallest words carry deep semiotic and theological significance.

How Far Does the Story Descend

But how far did this Story descend—not just to intersect but to interweave with our human narrative? The incarnation is not merely about God taking human form; it is about the Divine Author writing the very being of God into the messiest chapters of human existence, from our first cry to our final breath.

The First Chapter? Where did the author of this Story choose to open its earthly narrative: The Creator of the universe, whose imagination spun galaxies into being, chose to begin the Creator's cradle story in a stable. Not the quaint, clean structure of our Christmas pageants, but a first-century Palestinian cave where animals were kept. These stables were places of dirt, dung, and decay. Water was too precious to waste on regular cleaning; the pervasive stench of animal waste hung heavy in the air. The feeding troughs might be rinsed, but the floor remained thick with countless layers of organic matter. Let's spit it out: the cradle of the Christ child was a cesspit. This was no accidental setting. The Author of Life could have chosen any scene to bassinet the baby's entrance. Instead, God selected this place of primal filth for God's son's birth. The very first breaths of God-made-flesh were drawn in air heavy with the pungent smell of our earthly existence.

... there is no depth to which divine love will not go to reach us, to save us, to make us whole.

The Divine Story did not merely touch our story; it was immersed in its raw realities. As the first Adam emerged from the earth's clay, the second Adam entered a world no less primal-born amid the stench of livestock, laid in a dung-flecked manger's straw. Both began in lowliness: one shaped from dust, the other born in the dust and dross of human existence. From these depths, both Adam Alpha and Adam Omega would rise to revolutionize all of creation.

This divine descent finds its completion at Golgotha—a name derived from the Aramaic *"gulgulta,"* meaning "skull." Here, at the place of death, at a garbage dump where human remains were discarded, the circle of humiliation was completed. But even this was not the final indignity.

All four gospel writers, in an extraordinary act of preservation, record a detail that most would prefer to forget: the offering of the sponge. How many sermons have you heard on the sponge? Matthew 27:48 and Mark 15:36 mention a sponge soaked in sour wine on a stick, offered to Jesus. Luke 23:36 briefly states that soldiers offered Jesus sour wine. John 19:29 specifies that the sponge was placed on a branch of hyssop.

. . . this is a God who knows intimately the depths of human experience, who has touched and tasted and lived our reality in its most crude forms.

This was not mercy. This was mockery. The sponge was mounted on a hyssop branch (remember the Passover story and the blood on the doorposts, anyone?). These xylospongium's were the very implements used in Roman latrines as their version of toilet paper and cleaning brush. After use, these sponges on a stick, also called tersorium, would be rinsed in vinegar. This toilet sponge soaked in vinegar, this used Charmin wipe, was what was offered to the parched lips of the dying Son of God.

We have not even begun to comprehend this divine journey

from celestial glory to human grime without the story of the sponge. Here is the heart of God's love made manifest: The incarnation reveals a God who refuses to remain distant from our reality, who chooses instead to fully immerse Himself in the complete human experience—from the filth of birth to the degradation of death.

This is not a God who holds Himself aloof from human suffering and indignity. Rather, this is a God who knows intimately the depths of human experience, who has touched and tasted and lived our reality in its most crude forms. From stable to cross, from birth to death, God embraced it all, even the worst, transfiguring our understanding of both divinity and humanity.

In this descent, we find the ascent of human dignity. For if God Himself chose to be born among the dung and die among the refuse, then no human circumstance, no depth of degradation, lies beyond the reach of divine love and redemption. The very places we consider unclean become, through God's presence, sacred ground.

The Story Continues

This is the radical message of the incarnation: God's Story knows no limits, respects no boundaries, and recoils from no human mess. In choosing the stable for a cradle and embracing the cross in all its ugliness, Christ forever sanctified the lowest places of human existence, declaring that there is no chapter so stinky, no tale so tragic, no thought so ugly, that it lies beyond the reach of divine love and redemption.

In the end, this is our hope: not that we must write our way to God in our lifestories, but that God has already written the divine into our stories—meeting us exactly where we are, in whatever chapter we face. The stable and the cross stand as eternal passages in this greater Story, testifying that there is no depth to which divine love will not go to reach us, to save us, to make us whole.

And now, we too are invited to become part of this Story. Our lives, with all their soiled and screwed-up chapters, are being woven into this greater narrative of divine love. For the Story that began in eternity, that took flesh in a stable, that endured the cross, despised the shame, is still being written in the hearts and lives of all who embrace it.

> Let us fix our eyes on Jesus, the author and perfecter of our faith, who for the joy set before Him endured the cross, scorning its shame, and sat down at the right hand of the throne of God. Consider Him who endured such hostility from sinners, so that you will not grow weary and lose heart.
>
> —HEBREWS 12:2-3 NIV

Heart up. Are you ready?

ADVENT PRAYER

*I want to say this prayer for you . . . wherever you're at . . .
where you are . . . whatever your circumstances . . . whatever your lot.*

Dear God,

There's nothing too dirty that You can't redeem and make clean. There's nothing in our story that your Son's story doesn't cover.

There's no mess so deep that Your love cannot reach, No darkness so vast that Your light cannot pierce, No shame so heavy that Your grace cannot lift.

You chose a stable's filth to cradle Your Son, And a criminal's cross to complete His work.

Thank You, for writing Yourself into our messiest chapters. Thank you, for making sacred what we deemed unclean.

Thank you, for breathing dignity into our deepest degradation. Thank you, for turning our gory into glory.
O Come, O Come, Emmanuel, God WITH us, this Advent season. Maranatha. Amen.

WEEK ONE

EMBRACING THE STORY

Lectio Divina (Inspired Reading): As you read the passage below, take a deep breath and relax. Read slowly. Imagine yourself in the story. Let the words wash over you. Pay attention to how the Holy Spirit draws you in.

Matthew 1:18-25 ESV

Now the birth of Jesus Christ took place in this way. When his mother Mary had been betrothed to Joseph, before they came together she was found to be with child from the Holy Spirit. And her husband Joseph, being a just man and unwilling to put her to shame, resolved to divorce her quietly. But as he considered these things, behold, an angel of the Lord appeared to him in a dream, saying, "Joseph, son of David, do not fear to take Mary as your wife, for that which is conceived in her is from the Holy Spirit. She will bear a son, and you shall call his name Jesus, for he will save his people from their sins." All this took place to fulfill what the Lord had spoken by the prophet: 'Behold, the virgin shall conceive and bear a son . . . and they shall call his name Immanuel' (which means, God with us). When Joseph woke from sleep, he did as the angel of the Lord commanded him: he took his wife, but knew her not until she had given birth to a son. And he called his name Jesus.

INTERACTIVES

To continue your journey with reflections, questions, and activities, flip to the "Interactives: Prayerful Ponderings and Sacred Reflections" chapter toward the back of the book.

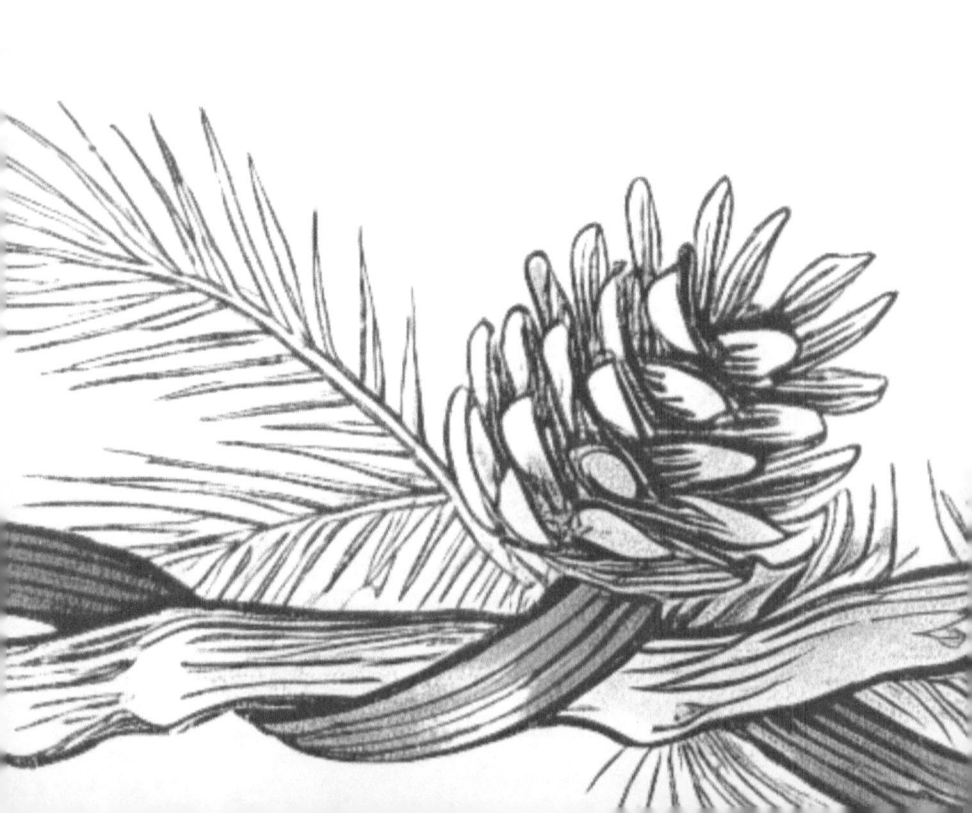

Week Two

THE MANGER MANIFESTO

WHEN YOU SAY "TAKE CARE" or "I care" or even "I Love You," these words can be transposed into the statement, "You matter to me."

"The Word became Flesh." In this divine alchemy, spirit doesn't just touch matter, it becomes matter. Every atom whispers of incarnation. The universe isn't just a stage for spirit; it's spirit's love letter written in stardust and gravity.

Einstein showed us how matter and space dance together. Matter curves space's canvas, while space choreographs matter's movement. But Christians glimpse an even deeper mystery: beyond **M**atter, **E**nergy, **S**pace, and **T**ime, lies Spirit. Spirit is just a fifth element, but the thread that weaves **MEST** into meaning.

Think of it: the Creator of quarks and quasars chose to speak through matter. When we say "Spirit Matters," we're making a cosmic pun. Spirit literally matters, transfigures into matter, and declares that all matter matters

The universe isn't just MEST. It's MEST[S], where Spirit is both the bracket that holds it all together and the force that infuses it all with purpose. In the incarnation, we see the ultimate proof: Spirit doesn't just animate matter; it becomes matter, blessing every physical thing with divine possibility.

> Spirit literally *matters*, transfigures into matter, and declares that all matter *matters*.

To say "I Matter" is to plant a seed. To declare "You Matter" is to nurture a garden. To proclaim "Lives Matter" like "Black Lives Matter" or "Disabled Lives Matter" or "Blue Lives Matter" or "Muslim Lives Matter" is to protect essential roots of our shared humanity. Yet these truths are but the foundation of a greater truth . . . and calling.

The static nature of "matter"—like a stone declaring its weight in the universe—must give way to the dynamic force of "mattering." For to matter is to simply be, but to be mattering is to become. It is the difference between a star's existence and its light reaching across galaxies. "Mattering" carries within it the pulse of purpose, the rhythm of impact, the dance of meaningful action. It commutes the noun of worth into the verb of legacy. When we shift from "I Matter" to "I'm Mattering," we move from claiming our space to actively shaping it: from asserting our value to creating value; from standing our ground to breaking new ground.

Am I "Mattering"?

This is the essence of our journey: not merely to occupy place or occupy *our* place in the universe, but to send ripples through it. Not simply to be counted, but to make every moment count. Not just to matter, but to be mattering – continuously, creatively, courageously.

For in mattering, we find not just our worth, but our mission in life. Not just our significance, but our calling. Not just our place in the story, but the point and power of the story itself. The Christmas story is the ultimate declaration of "You Matter" —God's profound statement to humanity through the Incarnation. When "the Word became Flesh," it wasn't just a spiritual concept becoming material; it was divine love taking the radical step of entering our material reality in its most vulnerable form: a baby born in a manger.

The divine "I CARE" echoed through the cosmos as angels announced this birth to shepherds, society's overlooked members. Their lives mattered enough for heaven to burst open with good news. The Magi's journey shows us that all cultures, all seekers matter. Their wisdom and gifts were welcomed at the manger.

In Jesus' birth, God didn't just say, "You Matter"—God demonstrated "mattering" in action. The static nature of divinity chose to enter the dynamic flow of human experience. Like stars sending light across galaxies, the light of Bethlehem's star wasn't just marking a location—it was actively guiding, illuminating, mattering across both space and time.

This first Christmas revolutionizes our understanding of mattering. Mary's "BE it unto ME" wasn't just acceptance of her worth. It was active participation in bringing hope into the world. Not just "LET IT BE" but "LET IT BE ME!" or "BE IT UNTO ME." Joseph's protection wasn't just acknowledging the child's importance; it was actively creating space for love to grow.

The manger scene itself embodies this distinction between "matter" and "mattering." The stable wasn't just occupying space. It was becoming a sanctuary. The swaddling clothes weren't just material. They were actively cradling divine love. Even the animals weren't just present—the donkey, the red heifer, the camel, the sheep—they were sharing their warmth, participating in the greatest story of hospitality ever told.

A World of Antimatter

Just as physicists discovered that for every particle of matter there exists its opposite—antimatter. We too encounter forces in our world that seek to negate worth, "You don't matter." "It doesn't matter." "Nothing matters." These are the dark antimatter messages that collide with human dignity, threatening to annihilate hope.

The Christmas story arose in a world full of such antimatter messages. A Roman Empire declaring that local lives didn't matter. A society telling a young unmarried mother she didn't matter. A home (we call it an inn) suggesting there was no room in the guest room, that these travelers didn't matter. Even

Herod's later actions would scream that innocent children didn't matter.

Instead, the divine "You Matter" proved more powerful than all the forces of negation.

But here's the miracle—when matter meets antimatter in physics, there's an explosion of pure energy. Similarly, when God's declaration of mattering met the world's antimatter messages, it didn't result in mutual destruction. Instead, the divine "You Matter" proved more powerful than all the forces of negation. A baby's cry pierced the darkness. Light shone in the shadows. Love converted a feeding trough into a cradle of revolution. Today, we still live in a world where antimatter messages abound.

"Black lives don't matter."
"Refugees don't matter."
"The poor don't matter."
"The elderly don't matter."
"The weak and wounded don't matter."

This isn't merely about end-of-life care or personal choice. It's about the fundamental question that echoes through every age: Who decides when a life has lost its worth? When suffering outweighs significance? When the burden becomes too great for the bearer—or for those who bear witness?

Perhaps nowhere is this arithmetic more stark than in the growing movement to redefine compassion itself. Across nations —from the cobblestone streets of old Europe to the familiar landscapes of our own Pacific Northwest—we're witnessing an unprecedented shift. What once was unthinkable has become policy, wrapped in gentle acronyms and careful language. MIND they call it in some places—Medically Induced Natural Death. MAID in others—Medical Assistance in Dying. The names are soft, clinical, but the message cuts through the euphemisms with surgical precision: some lives have reached their limit of mattering.

Yet Christmas reminds us that the ultimate power in the universe isn't destruction, but creation. Not antimatter, but mattering. When we declare "You Matter" in the face of "You don't," when we insist on the worth of the overlooked and undervalued, we participate in the same divine energy that turned a stable into a sanctuary and shepherds into evangelists.

> ... when we insist on the worth of the overlooked and undervalued, we participate in the same divine energy that turned a stable into a sanctuary and shepherds into evangelists.

Like Mary's Magnificat proclaiming that God "has filled the hungry with good things," our acts of mattering—feeding the hungry, welcoming the stranger, protecting the vulnerable—become antimatter's antidote. We don't fight antimatter with its own weapons. We metamorphize it through the persistent, powerful energy of love in action.

This Christmas, as forces of antimatter seem to gather strength—in war zones, in divided communities, in broken relationships—we're called to remember that the first Christmas was God's decisive response to all messages of "you don't matter." In choosing to become matter, to enter our material reality, God forever sealed the truth that everyone and everything matters. Not as an abstract principle, but as an active force changing the world one manger, one person, one moment of mattering at a time.

When we celebrate Christmas, we're not just remembering that God values matter—we're invited into the ongoing action of mattering. Like the shepherds, we're called not just to receive the good news, but to spread it. Like the Magi, we're called not just to witness the light, but to follow it and share our gifts.

ADVENT PRAYER

    Divine Creator of MATTER and Meaning,
    You who shaped the first Adam from clay
    and sent the second Adam to a manger of straw—
    we stand in awe of how You matter and make matter holy.

    And in Your hands, clay meets celestial straw
    to form the bricks from which Your kingdom rises.

    In a world heavy with antimatter messages,
    where voices cry "you don't matter" and "nothing matters,"

    You became matter itself—
    choosing the vulnerability of flesh,
    the warmth of wool,
    the roughness of wood,
    the cold of night,
    to declare that everything matters.

    Lord of the cosmos who taught matter to dance with space,
    who filled emptiness with stars and souls with purpose,
    help us move beyond merely mattering
    to the holy work of mattering:
    Like Mary's "Be it unto me,"
    Like Joseph's protective love,
    Like shepherds running to tell the news,
    Like Magi following Your light across deserts

Transfigure our static beings into dynamic becomings.
Turn our mangers into sanctuaries,
our presence into purpose,
our existence into essence.

In a world that would unmake Your children,
help us remake it with acts of love

until every soul knows its worth,
until angels bend near earth to touch their harps of gold,
until all the weary world rejoices,
until silent nights birth holy nights,
until mountains and hills break forth in singing,
until every heart prepares Him room,
until peace on earth rings out like bells,
until heaven and nature sing Your glory,
until all creation echoes Your eternal truth:

We matter because—You first mattered us.
In the name of the Word made Flesh,
who matters and makes all things matter,
Amen.

EMBRACING THE STORY

Lectio Divina (Inspired Reading): As you read the passage below, take a deep breath and relax. Read slowly. Imagine yourself in the story. Let the words wash over you. Pay attention to how the Holy Spirit draws you in.

Luke 1:26-38 ESV

In the sixth month the angel Gabriel was sent from God to a city of Galilee named Nazareth, to a virgin betrothed to a man whose name was Joseph, of the house of David. And the virgin's name was Mary. And he came to her and said, Greetings, O favored one, the Lord is with you! But she was greatly troubled at the saying, and tried to discern what sort of greeting this might be. And the angel said to her, Do not be afraid, Mary, for you have found favor with God. And behold, you will conceive in your womb and bear a son, and you shall call his name Jesus. He will be great and will be called the Son of the Most High. And the Lord God will give to him the throne of his father David, and he will reign over the house of Jacob forever, and of his kingdom there will be no end. And Mary said to the angel, "How will this be, since I am a virgin?" And the angel answered her, "The Holy Spirit will come upon you, and the power of the Most High will overshadow you; therefore the child to be born will be called holy—the Son of God. And behold, your relative Elizabeth in her old age has also conceived a son, and this is the sixth month with her who was called barren. For nothing will be impossible with God." And Mary said, "Behold, I am the servant of the Lord; let it be to me according to your word." And the angel departed from her.

INTERACTIVES

To continue your journey with reflections, questions, and activities, flip to the "Interactives: Prayerful Ponderings and Sacred Reflections" chapter toward the back of the book.

O come, O Bright and Morning Star,
and bring us comfort from afar!
Dispel the shadows of the night
and turn our darkness into light.

"O Come, O Come Emmanual"
hymn translated by J.M. Neale (1851)
Public Domain

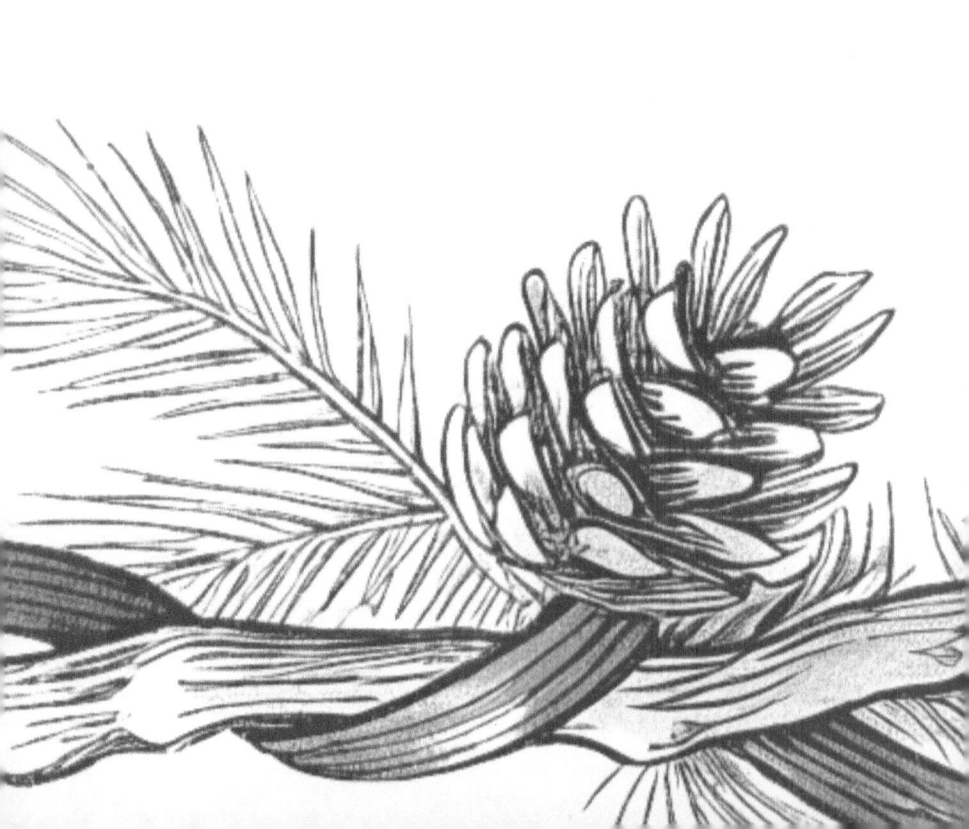

Week Three

THE SACRED DANCE OF SILENCE AND SONG

ARE YOU A "SILENT NIGHT" Christian or a "Jingle Bells" Christian? I am both, for the spirit moves in different rhythms through the sacred seasons. There are times for hushed contemplation and times when joy demands expression.

Silent Night or Jingle Bells?

In Eastertide, my Pentecostal heart emerges, and the "shouting Methodist" in my bones awakens. How can one remain quiet in the face of death's defeat, when the mystery of resurrection demands that we "Go Tell It On the Mountain"—a hymn that perhaps belongs more to Easter morning's triumph than to Christmas Eve's gentle wonder?

But when Christmas draws near, I find myself drawn to the ancient ways—to incense-filled sanctuaries and centuries-old liturgies, to the contemplative spirit of Eastern Orthodoxy. Christmas calls for silence, falling gentle as snow upon snow, inviting us into the profound stillness where the mystery of incarnation dwells.

In the echoing halls of Pilate's court, a question reverberates through the centuries: "What is truth?" The cosmic irony hangs thick as incense—Truth Himself, clothed in flesh and crowned with silence, stands before the questioner. This holy hush mirrors the stillness of that first Christmas night, creating a divine paradox: the eternal Word, through whom all things came into being, stands wordless. This sacred silence speaks volumes, just as a newborn's first breath in Bethlehem proclaimed God's presence more eloquently than a thousand sermons.

The shepherds understood this mystical language of silence as they knelt before the manger, their heartbeats synchronizing with the holy hush of that sacred night. No theological treatises were necessary, no explanations required. The presence itself was the present—Emmanuel, God dwelling among us, breathing softly in swaddling clothes.

In Pilate's hall, that same Truth stood robed in silence, offering not arguments but presence, not defense but divine love incarnate. From cradle to cross, Christ's most profound messages often came wrapped in silence. "Silent Night, Holy Night" becomes not merely a carol, but a key unlocking the mysteries of divine revelation. It is truly "The Gospel According to Silence,"[1] where Truth is not merely spoken but embodied, not merely heard but encountered in the sacred stillness of a heart made ready, like a manger, to receive its King.

. . . the sacred stillness of a heart made ready, like a manger to receive its King.

Truth, we discover at Christmas, is not an abstraction to be mastered but a Presence to be encountered. Like starlight falling softly on shepherd's fields, it requires not our intellect first, but our stillness. As Luigi Gioia beautifully observes, silence becomes "a sustained ability to be present . . . waiting lovingly and expectantly long enough for all the many layers of its epiphany to unfold."[2]

Christmas Poetry and Easter Prose

Christmas is poetry. Easter is prose. Poetry dwells in the sacred solitude where the soul dances alone with its thoughts. Prose celebrates in the communal feast where hearts and minds converge in shared story.

Christmas becomes poetry incarnate—with its contemplative moments, candlelight's soft glow, and snow's serene blanket, each element a verse in the poem of divine presence. Easter embodies prose—with its communal exultation, shared meals, and collective celebration of renewal, weaving a tapestry of human connection blessed by divine grace.

Easter Joy transcends mere happiness or contentment. It's not the casual cheer of "for he's a jolly good fellow", but the profound exultation of "my soul rejoices in the Lord" and the promise that "in your presence there is fullness of joy; at your right hand are pleasures forevermore" (Psalm 16:11) or "enter the joy of the Lord" (Matthew 25:21, 23). This joy harmonizes with both silence and stillness, though these are distinct gifts. Silence flows from the outside in. Stillness radiates from the inside out.

Silence comes as an external blessing—the absence of worldly clamor. We find it in dawn-touched forests, empty sanctuaries, or rooms recently vacated. Yet even in perfect silence, our internal world might churn with thoughts and emotions. Jacques-Bénigne Bossuet, the Bishop of Meaux (1681–1704), identified three sacred silences in his "Meditation on Silence": "the silence of rule, the silence of prudence in conversation, and the silence of patience in affliction." Our fractured world yearns for all three.

Stillness, however, wells up from within—a state of being rather than an environmental condition. One can find stillness in a bustling marketplace, a quiet center amid chaos. It's the settling of mental turbulence, the discovery of an inner calm that at-homes our relationship with the world.

This is why contemplatives can find peace even in noise.

The
silence
of Christmas
descends like
snow—from heaven
to earth. In the hush of
Christmas Eve streets,
when commerce **yields** to
c o n t e m p l a t i o n.
In the moment after the final carol
fades into candlelit darkness.
In the soft predawn hours when children dream
of morning's mysteries. This silence comes as the
world's gift, a precious respite from its constant clamor.
The stillness of Christmas rises like prayer—
from earth to heaven, In the quiet center we find when
we step away from the commercial whirl *to remember* the **holy**,
In the moment *we pause* to truly see the
light-adorned tree, In the deep
b r e a t h
we take
**when we set aside
our lists and agendas.**

This stillness is our gift to ourselves, a conscious choice to be present. Yet the Art of Stilling doesn't create a Still Life. As Steve Chase learned from a red-tailed hawk: "Every nerve and muscle was attentive, ready. Yet in her practiced flight, she was still—still to the wind, still to the earth, an anchor in the sky."[3] Or as Willie Nelson muses, in what he says is his favorite song he has written, "Still is Still Moving to Me."

Christmas uniquely invites both silence and stillness. The same night that brought silence to Bethlehem—no room at the inn, shepherds in quiet fields, a star hanging in the dark—also brought profound stillness: a mother contemplating her child, magi following their hearts, the world holding its breath at a moment of transfiguration.

We need both gifts. The outer silence creates space for reflection. The inner stillness allows us to fill that space with meaning. Together, they transfigure a holiday too often marked by hurry and noise into something closer to its original wonder—a time when both heaven and heart fall quiet enough to hear hope being born.

WEEK THREE

ADVENT PRAYER

Divine Mystery,
Who speaks in silence and moves in stillness,
Who came as Word yet rested wordless in a manger,
Draw us into Your sacred dance of presence.

In a world that fears silence,
Teach us the eloquence of hushed wonder.

In a season of endless noise, Grant us the courage to be still.

Like shepherds on that holy night,
May we know You in heartbeats and starlight,
In breaths between carols, In spaces between words.

LET OUR SOULS BE as mangers:
Empty enough to receive You, Quiet enough to hold You,
Still enough TO KNOW YOU.

Transfigure our celebrations and our solitude,
Until both our silence and our singing
Become prayers of presence,

And all our moments rest, Still in One PEACE. Amen.

EMBRACING THE STORY

Lectio Divina (Inspired Reading): As you read the passage below, take a deep breath and relax. Read slowly. Imagine yourself in the story. Let the words wash over you. Pay attention to how the Holy Spirit draws you in.

Luke 1:19-25 ESV

> And the angel answered him, I am Gabriel. I stand in the presence of God, and I was sent to speak to you and to bring you this good news. And behold, you will be silent and unable to speak until the day that these things take place, because you did not believe my words, which will be fulfilled in their time. And the people were waiting for Zechariah, and they were wondering at his delay in the temple. And when he came out, he was unable to speak to them, and they realized that he had seen a vision in the temple. And he kept making signs to them and remained mute. And when his time of service was ended, he went to his home. After these days his wife Elizabeth conceived, and for five months she kept herself hidden, saying, Thus the Lord has done for me in the days when he looked on me, to take away my reproach among people.

INTERACTIVES

To continue your journey with reflections, questions, and activities, flip to the "Interactives: Prayerful Ponderings and Sacred Reflections" chapter toward the back of the book.

"What Star Is This with Beams So Bright"
Author Charles Coffin (1736)

1. What star is this, with beams so bright,
Which shame the sun's less radiant light?
'Tis sent t' announce a new-born King,
Glad tidings of our God to bring.

2. 'Tis now fulfilled what God decreed:
"From Jacob shall a star proceed";
And lo! the eastern sages stand
To read in heav'n the Lord's command.

3. While outward signs the star displays,
An inward light the Lord conveys,
And urges them, with force benign,
To seek the Giver of the sign.

4. Oh, while the star of heav'nly grace
Invites us, Lord, to seek thy face,
May we no more that grace repel,
Or quench that light, which shines so well!

5. To God the Father, God the Son,
And Holy Spirit, Three in One,
May every tongue and nation raise
An endless song of thankful praise!

Week Four

THE FIRST CHRISTMAS CAROL

CHRISTMAS IS the story of curses turned into blessings—where exile becomes homecoming, darkness cradles light, and a feeding trough becomes a throne. In a world that cursed women with pain in childbirth, a young mother's labor delivers salvation. In a land crushed under foreign rule, the true King arrives—not with marching armies, but with infant murmurs. What was meant to humble becomes holy: shepherds become the first evangelists, a cattle stall becomes a cathedral, and death begins its long surrender to the child in the manger. The greatest curse —separation from God—becomes the greatest blessing: Emmanuel. God with us, now and forever.

Divine Withness

At Christmas, God hands us God's business card: the middle line in bold letters reads "WITH." Here, the divine witness of the Trinity's mutual dance—what theologians call perichoresis—extends to us. The God who eternally indwells now eternally abides. This presence transfigures every fragment of time into foreverness.

The Greek word perichoresis (περιχώρησις) comes from peri (around) and chorein (to make room, to contain, or to move forward). It shares a root with choreia, meaning "dance." Indeed, early theologians describe the Trinity as a divine dance of mutual indwelling—a circle of love and unity.

> Indeed, early theologians describe the Trinity as a divine dance of mutual indwelling—a circle of love and unity.

This brings us to the first Christmas carol. The angelic proclamation—"they shall call His name Emmanuel" (Matthew 1:23)—isn't just a name. It's a song. Like a carol's circular dance,

Emmanuel sings a moving circle of meaning: God-WITH-Us. The naming itself enacts what it proclaims: the first step in the eternal dance of divinity and humanity. The angel's later words to the shepherds—"Glory to God in the highest, and on earth peace . . . "—may be called the first Christmas carol in a traditional sense. But it's really the second. The first carol is the naming of Emmanuel. God's "middle name," declared as "WITH," initiates the divine choreography, where heaven and earth are joined.

Make us bearers of
Your light
in this world's
shadowed corners.

God WITH Us. Every carol sung since echoes that first sacred song, the "naming" carol. The Incarnation invites us all into the eternal dance: God with us, and us with God. *Us WITH God.* Even in moments of conflict, we can embody this divine "with-ness." When met with curses, we might respond as Barnabas would—with a gracious (if impish) grin and an echo of creation's first blessing: "Be fruitful and multiply." In this way, we join the eternal dance, turning curses into carols, hostility into harmony.

The Father and the Son and the Holy Spirit.
Oh blessed Trinity.
Unbegotten one, begotten one, regenerating one,
Oh blessed Trinity.
True Light, Light from light, true enlightening one.
Oh blessed Trinity.
Unseen invisibility, seen invisibility, unseen visibility.
Oh blessed Trinity.

—*PRAYER IN PRAISE OF THE TRINITY, BEDE,
(673-735)*

ADVENT PRAYER I

Holy One,
In this sacred season,
we marvel at Your
greatest gift—Your
presence with us,
Your divine "WITH."

We stand in awe of how You turn curses into blessings: Where there was exile, You make a home; Where there was darkness, You cradle light; Where there was a humble manger, You place Your throne.

Draw us into Your eternal dance, Where shepherds become messengers, Where stables turn into sanctuaries,
Where every moment
holds Your presence.

Emmanuel, God-with-us,
You who joined heaven and
earth in an infant's cry,
Draw us into Your circle of love—
The endless dance of Trinity
Now opened wide to all humanity.

Let us, like Mary, bear Your light;
Like shepherds, share Your story;
Like angels, sing Your praise;
Until every curse becomes a blessing,
And all creation joins Your dance of grace.

In the name of the Christ Child,
The One who makes Your "WITH" eternal,
Amen.

ADVENT PRAYER II

Father of Light, In the hush of winter nights,
When stars pierce through darkness
And frost rims the world in silver,
We remember Your coming.

Not in THUNDER,
Not in EARTHQUAKE,
Not in STORM,
But in a mother's
whispered
lullaby,
In a newborn's first breath,
In the quiet wonder of shepherds
Standing beneath Your luminous sky.

Teach us to find You,
In life's tender places—
Where hope flickers like candlelight,
Where love makes a home in unlikely spaces,
Where grace falls
as soft as snow.

Let us carry Your presence
As Mary carried Your Son:
With reverence, With courage,
With hearts made W I D E by W O N D E R.
Make us bearers of Your light

In this world's shadowed corners.
Let our lives become carols,
Our days become prayers,
Until earth and heaven
Meet in endless morning.
Through Christ, the Dawn of all our nights,
Amen.

EMBRACING THE STORY

Lectio Divina (Inspired Reading): As you read the passage below, take a deep breath and relax. Read slowly. Imagine yourself in the story. Let the words wash over you. Pay attention to how the Holy Spirit draws you in.

Luke 1:39-56 ESV

In those days Mary arose and went with haste into the hill country, to a town in Judah . . . And when Elizabeth heard the greeting of Mary, the baby leaped in her womb. And Elizabeth was filled with the Holy Spirit, and she exclaimed with a loud cry, Blessed are you among women, and blessed is the fruit of your womb! And why is this granted to me that the mother of my Lord should come to me? For behold, when the sound of your greeting came to my ears, the baby in my womb leaped for joy.

And blessed is she who believed that there would be a fulfillment of what was spoken to her from the Lord. And Mary said, My soul magnifies the Lord, and my spirit rejoices in God my Savior, for he has looked on the humble estate of his servant. For behold, from now on all generations will call me blessed; for he who is mighty has done great things for me, and holy is his name. And his mercy is for those who fear him from generation to generation. He has shown strength with his arm; he has scattered the proud in the thoughts of their hearts; he has brought down the mighty from their thrones and exalted those of humble estate; he has filled the hungry with good things, and the rich he has sent away empty. He has helped his servant Israel, in remembrance of his mercy, as he spoke to our fathers, to Abraham and to his offspring forever.

INTERACTIVES

To continue your journey with reflections, questions, and activities, flip to the "Interactives: Prayerful Ponderings and Sacred Reflections" chapter toward the back of the book.

Christmas Eve

O HOLY NIGHT

IN THE DEPTHS OF WINTER, when darkness wraps around us like a velvet cloak, we gather on this holy night. The world holds its breath, awaiting once again the miracle that occurred in Bethlehem's darkness. Outside our windows, the night unfolds its ancient mystery, just as it did over two thousand years ago when shepherds stood watch over their flocks.

O Holy Night

"O holy night," we sing, and perhaps never before have we understood the holiness of darkness quite like this. Michelangelo, that master who painted light emerging from darkness, once wrote: "Only in darkness can men fully be themselves, and therefore night is holier than day."[1] What wisdom lies in these words, what truth about our own nature!

Think of how a seed must first push down into the dark earth before it can reach toward the light. The deeper the roots grow in darkness, the higher the plant can stretch toward the sun. "No plant," Michelangelo tells us, "has half the worth of man." If even the simplest flower requires darkness to grow, how much more do we, with our complex souls and yearning hearts, need these sacred moments of holy darkness?

God Himself, the psalmist tells us, "has made darkness his secret place" (Psalm 18:11). On this night of nights, we remember how the divine chose to enter our world not in the blazing sun of noon, but in the quiet darkness of midnight. The King of Kings arrived not in a palace filled with light, but in the shadows of a humble stable, where animals dozed and stars kept their distant vigil.

Louis Armstrong understood something of this mystery when he sang of "bright blessed day, and dark sacred night." In the sacred dark, we become most fully ourselves. Like Mary, pondering these things in her heart, darkness gives us space to wonder, to question, to grow. In the shadows, we can acknowledge our doubts, our fears, our deepest longings—those things we sometimes hide even from ourselves in the glare of day.

> The people who walked in darkness have seen a great light; those who dwelt in a land of deep darkness, on them has light shone.
>
> —ISAIAH 9:2 ESV

"The people who walked in darkness," Isaiah proclaimed, "have seen a great light." But first they had to walk in darkness. First they had to learn to trust the night, to let it teach them, transfigure them, prepare them for the light to come. Just as a photographer needs a darkroom to develop images, our souls need darkness to develop wisdom.

On this holy night, we sit in darkness not to escape the light, but to prepare for it. Like seeds in winter soil, like children in the womb, like Christ in the manger, we grow in these sacred shadows. The darkness of this night is not empty. It is pregnant with possibility, laden with promise, holy with anticipation.

And so we wait, and watch, and wonder. Will you let the darkness do its holy work in you? Will you, this Christmas Eve, open yourself to a noctuary experience: the midnight thrill of being alive to all of life? For soon, very soon, a child will cry out in the night, and everything will change. The light will come. But first—this holy darkness, this sacred night, this blessed time of growing down so that we might grow up, of reaching deep so that we might reach high. "O holy night," we sing, and in the darkness, we become ready for the light.

CHRISTMAS EVE PRAYER

Eternal God, keeper of sacred mysteries,
On this holy night, we pause in the blessed darkness that wraps around us like Your loving embrace.

As nature holds its breath and stars keep their ancient vigil, we too wait in holy anticipation, just as shepherds did on that first Christmas Eve.

In this sacred darkness,
we plant ourselves like seeds in Your winter soil.
Let our roots grow deep in these quiet hours of contemplation, that our spirits might reach higher toward Your light.

Like Mary, we ponder the mysteries in our hearts, finding in these shadows the space to wonder, to question, and to grow.

Lord of the midnight hour,
You who made darkness Your secret place,
we remember how You chose to enter our world
not in blazing noon, but in the quiet depths of night.

In a humble stable's shadows,
You revealed Your greatest light.
As we wait in this pregnant darkness, laden with possibility, open our hearts to its holy work within us.
Turn our doubts into wonder,

our fears into faith, our longing into love.

Like the people who walked in darkness before seeing
Your great light, prepare us for the miracle about to manifest.

And when the Christ child's cry pierces this sacred night,
may we be ready—souls deepened by darkness,
hearts opened by anticipation, spirits prepared to receive Your transfiguring light.

In the name of the One who hallowed the night, and for whom darkness is as day, Amen.

EMBRACING THE STORY

Lectio Divina (Inspired Reading): As you read the passage below, take a deep breath and relax. Read slowly. Imagine yourself in the story. Let the words wash over you. Pay attention to how the Holy Spirit draws you in.

Luke 2:1-14 ESV

And it came to pass in those days that a decree went out from Caesar Augustus that all the world should be registered. This census first took place while Quirinius was governing Syria. So all went to be registered, everyone to his own city. Joseph also went up from Galilee, out of the city of Nazareth, into Judea, to the city of David, which is called Bethlehem, because he was of the house and lineage of David, to be registered with Mary, his betrothed wife, who was with child. So it was, that while they were there, the days were completed for her to be delivered.

And she brought forth her firstborn Son, and wrapped Him in swaddling cloths, and laid Him in a manger, because there was no room for them in the inn.

Now there were in the same country shepherds living out in the fields, keeping watch over their flock by night. And behold, an angel of the Lord stood before them, and the glory of the Lord shone around them, and they were greatly afraid. Then the angel said to them, "Do not be afraid, for behold, I bring you good tidings of great joy which will be to all people. For there is born to you this day in the city of David a Savior, who is Christ the Lord. And this will be the sign to you: You will find a Babe wrapped in swaddling cloths, lying in a manger." And suddenly there was with the angel a multitude of the heavenly host praising God and saying: "Glory to God in the highest, And on earth peace, goodwill toward men!"

... in the darkness, we become ready for the light.

Christmas Day
THE ENCHANTMENT OF WONDER

IN THIS SYMPHONY OF DECEMBER, where silver bells ring through frost-kissed air and starlight dances on windowpanes, we're invited into a realm of wonder that transcends the ordinary. The very atmosphere whispers secrets, steeped in pine and cinnamon, beckoning us beyond the mundane rush of shopping lists and deadlines.

Maybe the two people that have most shaped our Christmas celebrations are Charles Dickens and John Wanamaker. Wanamaker's grand vision in Philadelphia was for commerce to wear cathedral robes. His department store stood as a testament to transformed spaces—where stained glass caught the light and cast rainbow shadows on marble floors, where men instinctively removed their hats as if crossing a sacred threshold. Here, shopping wasn't merely transaction; it was transformation, each purchase wrapped in reverence, each moment gilded with awe.

Yet even as we marvel at such architectural enchantment, we're drawn to an older, simpler wonder. For beneath the cascade of twinkling lights and between the lines of carols sung, there whispers an ancient story—of a starlit night in Bethlehem, where divinity chose humanity's embrace. This narrative, so familiar yet ever new, remains the heart of all our celebrations, the quiet center in our woozy, whirling world of festivities.

The Greatest Gift arrived not in gilded paper but in humble cloth, not in a merchant's palace but in a borrowed manger. This profound simplicity calls to us still, inviting us to discover wonder in unexpected places. It challenges us to see beyond the glitter, to find magic in acts of ordinary kindness, to recognize holiness in human hearts.

We celebrate today letting each gift shared echo that first Christmas gift. Let our homes become sacred spaces not through grandeur, but through love. Let our gatherings shimmer not just with candlelight, but with compassion. "Freely you have received, freely give," the Bible says. We who have freely received such wonder are called to freely give–not just presents, but presence; not just things, but thoughtfulness; not just celebration, but transfiguration.

> We who have freely received such wonder are called to freely give–not just presents, but presence; not just things, but thoughtfulness; not just celebration, but transfiguration.

In this season of lights and shadows, of feasts and fasting, of receiving and giving, may we become bearers of wonder. May our lives tell the story anew, each act of kindness a star pointing the way, each moment of generosity a note in the eternal carol of love.

For in the end, the true enchantment of this season lies not in what we can buy, but in who we can become–mirrors reflecting divine love, vessels overflowing with grace, people forever changed by the simple, stunning truth that Love chose to dwell among us that first Christmas. And still does.

The wonder deepens when we recognize that this indwelling love chose not just to dwell among us, but to be wounded for us. In the great paradox of divine love, the very wounds that mark our human condition become the channels through which healing flows. Our brokenness becomes the meeting place with God's wholeness, our wounds the sacred ground where wonder and wisdom converge.

God's design for humanity is wholeness, yet we find ourselves immersed in a culture of woundedness. The gospel story unfolds as a divine drama of transfiguration from a state of woundedness into a shalom of flourishing. But how does God do this? Through a sacred grafting—a union of wound to wound. God's touch upon our mortal wounds with sacred wounds initiates this healing. In the five wounds of Christ on the cross, suffering transcends its own nature, becoming a channel of redemption.

These five holy wounds, carried into glory, now pulse with redemptive power, each beat echoing love's triumph over death. The very marks of His mortality now mark our path to eternal life—testimonies of love's costliest victory.

Even the heavenly hosts, their gazes ablaze, are humbled by the radiant mystery of these wounds, their brilliance almost blinding in its intensity of love. To live Christ is to partake in this sacred alchemy, where wounds become windows, darkness gives birth to light, death surrenders to the dance of life, and mystery blossoms into the dawn's brightest star. As the hymn "Diademata" so eloquently proclaims in stanza three:

> *Crown him the Lord of love;*
> *behold his hands and side,*
> *rich wounds, yet visible above,*
> *in beauty glorified;*
> *no angels in the sky can fully bear that sight,*
> *but downward bends their burning eye*
> *at mysteries so bright.*[1]

The luminous mystery shines from beginning to end. The swaddling cloths that bound the infant Jesus foreshadowed the burial linens that would wrap his wounded body. The wood of the manger prefigured the wood of the cross. His first bed was a limestone manger, just as his last bed was a limestone slab. Even the myrrh brought by the Magi pointed to his death—it was an embalming spice. The humble stable where he was born mirrored the silent tomb where he would be laid.

Both narratives intertwine divine vulnerability. In his birth, God became touchable. In his death, God became wounded.

CHRISTMAS DAY

The incarnation begins what the crucifixion completes: God taking on human fragility to heal our brokenness.

> Let The Mystery Shine, people.
> Let The Mystery Shine, church.
> Let Thy Mystery Shine!

CHRISTMAS DAY PRAYER

Divine Creator,
In this sacred moment between anticipation and fulfillment,
WE PAUSE
in wonder before You.

As silver bells ring through December nights
and starlight graces our windowpanes,
open our eyes to the holy that dwells within the ordinary.

WE CONFESS
how easily we are caught in the swirl of celebrations,
how readily we mistake glitter for glory.

Yet even now,
You call us back to that first Christmas night,
when majesty chose a manger
and eternity stepped into time.

Thank You for the gift of Your presence—
not wrapped in gilded paper, but in swaddling clothes;
not announced in merchant halls, but in shepherd's fields.
May this profound simplicity remake us anew.
Grant us hearts to see beyond the surface of our celebrations
to their sacred center.

Let each gift we give echo Your great gift to us.

Make our homes holy not through grandeur, but through love;
our gatherings rich not through abundance, but through grace.

As we have freely received such wonder, help us freely give—not just presents, but presence; not just things, but thoughtfulness.

Let every act of kindness be a STAR guiding others to Your love, every gesture of generosity a note in the eternal carol of grace.

Transfigure us into bearers of Your light, vessels of Your love, people forever changed by the simple, stunning truth that You chose to dwell among us—and still do.
In humble gratitude we pray, Amen.

The swaddling cloths that bound the infant Jesus foreshadowed the burial linens that would wrap his wounded body.

EMBRACING THE STORY

Lectio Divina (Inspired Reading): As you read the passage below, take a deep breath and relax. Read slowly. Imagine yourself in the story. Let the words wash over you. Pay attention to how the Holy Spirit draws you in.

Luke 2:15-20 ESV

> When the angels went away from them into heaven, the shepherds said to one another, "Let us go over to Bethlehem and see this thing that has happened, which the Lord has made known to us." And they went with haste and found Mary and Joseph, and the baby lying in a manger. And when they saw it, they made known the saying that had been told them concerning this child. And all who heard it wondered at what the shepherds told them. But Mary treasured up all these things, pondering them in her heart. And the shepherds returned, glorifying and praising God for all they had heard and seen, as it had been told them.

INTERACTIVES

To continue your journey with reflections, questions, and activities, flip to the "Interactives: Prayerful Ponderings and Sacred Reflections" chapter toward the back of the book.

"O Morning Star, How Fair and Bright"

Author: Philipp Nicolai (1599); Translator: Catherine Winkworth

Come heavenly Brightness, Light divine,
and deep within my heart now shine,
there make yourself an altar!
Fill me with joy and strength to be
your member, joined eternally
in love that cannot falter;
Longing for you does possess me;
turn and bless me;
Here in sadness
eye and heart long for your gladness.

Hogmanay—New Year Beginning

WHEN THE SAINTS GO HOBBLING IN—LIVING AS BOTH ANSWER AND MYSTERY

HAPPY HOGMANAY![1]

As the new year begins, I'm thinking of Scotland, one of my ancestral homes, and its unique Hogmanay celebrations. From the tradition of "first-footing," symbolizing the warmth and welcome we extend to friends, family, and strangers, to the singing of "Auld Lang Syne"–"We'll tak' a cup o' kindness yet, for auld lang syne"–Hogmanay is a time for reflection and connection.

A Time for Reflection and Connection

The very word "Hogmanay" itself, with its fascinating etymology hinting at French, Gaelic, and Norse influences, speaks to Scotland's rich and layered past. It's a celebration of hospitality that touches the heart, torchlighting the future with memories of the past and the promise of what's to come.

In this tender moment between the old and the new, let us "first-foot" to raise this cup of kindness together—its warmth shared between old friends and new souls alike. With each sip of this sacred communion, may we discover the courage to be kind when our hearts resist, the wisdom to forgive when wounds run deep, and the grace to extend both to familiar faces and strangers. Here's to a year where kindness illuminates every heart and hallows every home.

In my childhood, the Sweet family welcomed each New Year on bent knees. Our "Watchnight Services" were sacred farewells to the old year, wrapped in prayers of repentance and forgiveness, while we heralded the new with petitions of hope. Our parents would chide us for a "bum kneel"—that halfway genuflection that never quite reached the ground. They remembered our circuit-rider ancestors who braved with their horses snow, wind, sleet, and sub-zero temperatures to preach the gospel, and whose knee-prints sometimes froze in winter snow, final testimonies that their last earthly breaths were spent in prayer.

Think of those saints who hobbled their way to glory—some bent with age, others worn from life's journey, and still others from spending countless hours on their knees. They showed us something beautiful: that our deepest worship often flows not from our strength, but from our willingness to be weak.

There's this wonderful quote that's echoed through the centuries, from a fourth-century monk named Evagrius: "If you are a theologian, you will pray truly, and if you pray truly, you will be a theologian." Later, Hans Urs von Balthasar would call this "kneeling theology"—this beautiful idea that faith grows tallest when we bow lowest.

But here's the fascinating thing: this "kneeling theology" isn't just about physically getting on our knees. Take the orant position, the only prayer posture we know for sure that Evagrius used. Picture someone standing with their face toward heaven, eyes wide open, arms raised with palms facing outward. It's beautifully contradictory: it looks like surrender (think "hands up!") but it's actually a stance of bold readiness.

Fresco from the Catacomb of Priscilla in Rome, showing an early Christian orant figure—public domain.

Those early Christians took what looked like submission and turned it into their own quiet rebellion, facing down the powers of their world with humble hearts but alert minds, standing firm while remaining open to grace. It wasn't until the eighth-century that Christians started praying with clasped hands or hands held close to their bodies. Maybe it's time we gave the orant another try.

Prayer Aware

As we cross this threshold into a new year, two profound truths intertwine like ancient melodies in sacred harmony. First: you are not merely one who prays—you are yourself an answer to prayer. Second: you stand as a steward of divine mysteries. Let these twin awarenesses settle into your kneeling spirit like morning dew on waiting earth.

> First: you are not merely one who prays—you are yourself an answer to prayer. Second: you stand as a steward of divine mysteries. Let these twin awarenesses settle into your kneeling spirit like morning dew on waiting earth.

Jesus favored brevity in spoken prayer. The Lord's Prayer requires but thirty seconds to voice. The tax collector's humble plea—"God, be merciful to me, a sinner" (Luke 18:13)—stands among Scripture's briefest prayers, yet Jesus held it up as exemplary. His explicit preference for direct, unadorned prayer rings clear in his warning against "vain repetitions" (Matthew 6:7-8) and his criticism of those who "for a pretense make long prayers" (Mark 12:40). Simplicity of prayer is the ultimate maturity of faith and sophistication of soul.

Yet Jesus also demonstrated the sacred place of sustained intercession. He spent whole nights wrapped in prayer's embrace

(Luke 6:12). His Gethsemane vigil stretched long into darkness (Matthew 26:36-44). His most extensive recorded prayer—the High Priestly Prayer of John 17—takes but a few minutes to speak aloud, yet spans eternity in its scope. In this prayer, Jesus first lifts Himself to the Father (verses 1-5), then his disciples (verses 6-19), and finally reaches across time to embrace all future believers (verses 20-26).

Love forms the prayer's crescendo: "that the love you have for me may be in them" (John 17:26). Here beats the heart of gospel truth: *The Father's boundless love for Jesus, Jesus' love flowing forth in prayer, That same love, now dwelling within you.*

In the words of sixteenth-century Spanish Reformer Teresa of Avila, "Prayer does not lie in thinking much but in loving much."

Psalm 46 was a lifelong inspiration for another sixteenth-century Reformer, Martin Luther. The psalm opens with the declaration "God is our refuge and strength, a very present help in trouble" (Psalm 46:1). This truth so moved Luther that he penned his most enduring hymn, "A Mighty Fortress is Our God," as a powerful meditation on its themes.

The psalm reveals a crucial theological distinction—God is not merely a handyman helper, but our constant refuge and dwelling place. The Hebrew emphasizes God's immediate accessibility, pointing to God's faithful, abiding presence that sustains us through every circumstance. Just as Luther found courage in these words during the tumultuous years of the Protestant Reformation, the psalm continues to remind us that our security lies not in God's occasional intervention, but in God's eternal, unchanging presence. God is not our present helper to do our bellman bidding, but our abiding presence. Our help is in God's presence.

The early church fathers painted varied perspectives on prayer's proper length. Origen (third-century) emphasized quality over duration. John Chrysostom (fourth-century) advocated brief, frequent prayers scattered like seeds throughout the day. Fourth-century African theologian St. Augustine found in the Lord's Prayer a complete template while acknowledging space for longer expressions of devotion.

Yet the evidence suggests Jesus prescribed not duration but disposition: Sincerity's quiet truth over showmanship's empty echo—Quality's deep well over quantity's shallow stream—Heart's genuine cry over form's hollow shell.

> Jesus prescribed not duration but disposition: Sincerity's quiet truth over showmanship's empty echo—Quality's deep well over quantity's shallow stream—Heart's genuine cry over form's hollow shell.

Two millennia past, in a Jerusalem upper room, Jesus offered his own variation of the Lord's Prayer that still ripples through time: "I pray also for those who will believe in me through their message . . ." (John 17:20). In that eternal moment, you were known. You were seen. The Divine Eye beheld you here, now, where you are sitting or standing, and you were wrapped in prayer's embrace.

You were also entrusted with precious cargo—what Paul would name "the mysteries of God" (1 Corinthians 4:1). These mysteries transcend mere doctrine; they are living relationships awaiting embrace. They find their fulfillment in Christ Himself (Colossians 2:2), revealing history's greatest love story: how the Infinite became an infant, donning our humanity, to bridge heaven and earth. Through Christ, ancient mysteries step into light—not as lessons for the mind, but as a divine dance of relationship inviting our participation.

You stand within this Circle of Divine Love, therefore:

- Rest in the Father's perfect love for Jesus.
- Embrace Jesus' love that prompted His prayer.
- Welcome this same divine love dwelling within.
- Stand as living testimony to love's enduring power.
- You are living proof that God hears and answers prayer.

Remember Jesus' words: "The harvest is plentiful but the workers are few. Ask the Lord of the harvest, therefore, to send out workers into his harvest field" (Matthew 9:37-38). As this new year dawns, never forget: You are both answer to prayer and steward of its ongoing mystery. Each relationship you nurture, each divide you bridge, each moment spent in wonder at God's love, weaves into this unfolding tapestry.

NEW YEAR PRAYER

You crown the year with your bounty, and your carts overflow with abundance.

—PSALM 65:11 NIV

Thank you, Jesus, for seeing me across time's vast expanse,
For weaving me into your eternal prayer,
For entrusting me with your sacred mysteries.

Thank you that I step not into newness alone,
But continue in the stream of your eternal purpose.

Let me live this year as both answer and steward,
Where doctrine blossoms into devotion
And theology flowers into testimony
Of a love that knows no bounds.

DAILY PRACTICES (RESOLVES NOT RESOLUTIONS) FOR A NEW YEAR:

As each day unfolds:

- Remember you continue an ancient story rather than beginning anew

- Embrace your dual role as answer to prayer and keeper of sacred mysteries
- Seek divine love's fingerprints in unexpected places
- Let these mysteries of relationship with God, others, self, and creation—guide and sustain you

HOGAMANY NEW YEAR BLESSING

May this New Year
deepen your awareness of your place
in God's unfolding love story.

May you discover anew these living mysteries,
not as principles to master but as relationships to cherish.

May every act of faith,
every expression of love,
every step of obedience echo both answer to Jesus' prayer and
stewardship of His mysteries.

Let faith's mysteries embrace you,
prayer's certainty ground you,
and divine love's wonder fill you in every moment ahead.

For you are not merely speaking prayers—you embody their answer. You are not simply studying mysteries—you are their living vessel.

Welcome to the New Year, beloved answer to prayer and steward of sacred mysteries.

EMBRACING THE STORY

Lectio Divina (Inspired Reading): As you read the passage below, take a deep breath and relax. Read slowly. Imagine yourself in the story. Let the words wash over you. Pay attention to how the Holy Spirit draws you in.

Matthew 2: 7-12 ESV

> Then Herod summoned the wise men secretly and ascertained from them what time the star had appeared. And he sent them to Bethlehem, saying, "Go and search diligently for the child, and when you have found him, bring me word, that I too may come and worship him." After listening to the king, they went on their way. And behold, the star that they had seen when it rose went before them until it came to rest over the place where the child was. When they saw the star, they rejoiced exceedingly with great joy. And going into the house, they saw the child with Mary his mother, and they fell down and worshiped him. Then, opening their treasures, they offered him gifts, gold and frankincense and myrrh. And being warned in a dream not to return to Herod, they departed to their own country by another way.

INTERACTIVES

To continue your journey with reflections, questions, and activities, flip to the "Interactives: Prayerful Ponderings and Sacred Reflections" chapter toward the back of the book.

Interactives

PRAYERFUL PONDERINGS AND SACRED REFLECTIONS

WEEK ONE INTERACTIVES: FROM GLORY TO GRIME

1. *The Power of Prepositions:* Reflect on the significance of prepositions in the biblical narrative, particularly "with" and "in." How do these relational words shape your understanding of God's presence in your life?

2. *The Incarnation as Solidarity:* How does the concept of "withness" in the Incarnation challenge or deepen your understanding of God's relationship with humanity?

3. *From Glory to Grime:* Consider the contrast between the divine glory and the earthly grime of Jesus' birth and death. What does this contrast reveal about God's character and love?

4. *The Significance of the Stable:* Why do you think God chose a stable, a place of dirt and decay, as the birthplace of Jesus? What message does this convey about God's attitude toward human imperfection?

5. *The Story of the Sponge:* Reflect on the symbolism of the sponge offered to Jesus on the cross. How does this detail underscore the depth of God's identification with human suffering?

6. *Divine Love and Redemption:* How does the Incarnation, particularly Jesus' birth and death, inform and confirm your understanding of divine love and redemption?

7. Human Dignity and Divine Love: Consider how the Incarnation elevates human dignity. How does this impact your perception of yourself and others?

8. God's Presence in the Messy: Where in your life do you feel like you're in a "messy" or difficult situation? How does the Incarnation's message of God's presence in the messy encourage or challenge you?

9. Embracing the Story: As you reflect on the Incarnation's narrative, how are you invited to become part of this greater Story of divine love? What steps can you take to more fully embody this Story in your daily life?

WEEK TWO INTERACTIVES: THE MANGER MANIFESTO

1. Divine Incarnation: How does the concept of "The Word became Flesh" change your understanding of the relationship between the spiritual and the material? How does this idea affect your daily interactions with the physical world?

2. Mattering vs. Matter: What's the difference between saying "I matter" and "I'm mattering"? How can this distinction influence personal growth and societal change?

3. The Cosmic Pun: Reflect on the phrase "Spirit matters." How does this play on words deepen your appreciation for both the spiritual and physical aspects of existence?

4. *Antimatter in Society:* What are some modern "antimatter messages" in society that negate human worth? How can we counter these messages with acts of affirmation and love?

5. *The Manger as Sanctuary:* In what ways does the metamorphosis of a manger into a sanctuary for Jesus reflect the potential for any space to become sacred through acts of love and inclusion?

6. *Active Participation:* How does Mary's response, "Be it unto me," inspire you to actively participate in the unfolding of hope or change in your community or personal life?

7. *The Power of Mattering:* Discuss how the idea of "mattering" can be applied to social justice movements like "Black Lives Matter." How does this concept empower collective action?

8. *Evolving Understanding of Care:* In light of contemporary practices like MAID (Medical Assistance in Dying), how should we redefine care to ensure it aligns with the message of "You Matter"?

9. *Christmas as a Call to Action:* How does the Christmas story challenge you to move from passive acknowledgment of human worth to active engagement in making everyone feel they matter? What concrete actions can you take to spread this message?

WEEK THREE INTERACTIVES: THE SACRED DANCE OF SILENCE AND SONG

1. Iron and Light: With every light of day, we strike the iron into swords or ploughshares, we forge the ore into weapon systems or living centers, we hammer away at destruction or construction, we worship at the altar of war or peace. But we cannot escape either the light of day or the iron of life, since iron is the building block of blood, the liquid of life that brings oxygen to the tissues of the body.

Dag Hammarskjöld was one of the towering figures of the twenty-century. The second Secretary-General of the UN, he conceived a Meditation Room "dedicated to silence" (in 1952) at the Headquarters Building which was built around a solid block of iron ore, with shafts of light striking the altar of iron at different angles throughout the day.[1]

2. Sing the Story: Join together for a little Christmas caroling, sacred soundscapes of both Silence and Stillness. Sing together songs like:

- "Wait for the Lord" (based on Psalm 27) - This song encourages patience and silence in waiting for God's presence.
- "O Come, O Come Emmanuel" - Contains themes of waiting and longing to create a contemplative atmosphere.
- "Silent Night" - This beloved carol's opening lines, "Silent night, holy night, all is calm, all is bright," evoke a sense of peaceful stillness.
- "It Came Upon a Midnight Clear" - The line—"And in despair I bowed my head; There is no peace on earth, I said—creates a moment of somber silence.

- "The First Noel" - "And all around the cottage bright, shone round the starry light," implies a quiet, serene scene.
- "Winter Snow" (Audrey Assad) - "You came like a winter snow/Quiet and soft and slow/Falling from the sky in the night/To the earth below."

Now sing together some sacred soundscapes of joy and gladness:

- "Carol of the Bells"
- "Ring the Bells"
- "I Heard the Bells on Christmas Day" (based on a Longfellow poem)
- "Ding Dong Merrily on High"
- "Silver Bells"
- "O Come All Ye Faithful, Joyful and Triumphant"

After listening to and singing both contemplative carols and joyful Christmas songs, which pieces speak most deeply to you? How do different sacred music styles help you connect with different aspects of your faith? When do you find yourself drawn to each type?

3. *Silence and Stillness:* The meditation suggests that "silence is from the outside in" while "stillness is from the inside out." Reflect on a time when you experienced each of these. How were they different? Which do you find more challenging to achieve?

4. *Poetry & Prose:* If Christmas is poetry and Easter is prose, how does this metaphor help you understand these two sacred

seasons differently? Which season's "language" comes more naturally to you in your life of faith?

5. *Silence Reflection:* Reflect on the three types of silence Bossuet identified: "the silence of rule, the silence of prudence in conversation, and the silence of patience in affliction." Which of these do you find most relevant to your life right now? Which does our community most need? A parallel is drawn between Christ's silence before Pilate and the quiet of the nativity. How does this connection between Christmas and Good Friday shape your understanding of divine presence? What does it tell us about how God chooses to communicate?

6. *The Presence of Truth:* If Truth is "not an abstraction to be grasped but a Presence to be encountered," how does this perspective challenge or enhance your approach to faith? Can you share an experience where you encountered truth through presence rather than explanation?

7. *Cultivating Stillness:* Reflect on the image of the red-tailed hawk being "still to the wind, still to the earth, an anchor in the sky." How might this kind of dynamic stillness differ from mere inactivity? What would it look like to cultivate this quality in your whole life?

8. *Silent Night & Jingle Bells:* I contrast being a "Silent Night Christian" with being a "Jingle Bells Christian." But I claim to be both. Rather than choosing between them, how might embracing both enhance your faith journey? What might each approach have to teach the other?

WEEK FOUR INTERACTIVES: THE FIRST CHRISTMAS CAROL

1. *God's WITH:* The prayer begins with a focus on God's "WITH." What significance do you find in emphasizing God's presence rather than God's power or other divine attributes? How might this shape our understanding of Christmas?

2. *Journey through Transfiguration:* Throughout the meditation, there are transfigurations: "curses into blessings," "exile into homecoming," "darkness cradles light." Which of these paradoxes resonates most deeply with your own faith journey, and why?

3. *Divine Dance:* The prayer references the "endless dance of Trinity" being "opened wide to all humanity." How do you understand this invitation to participate in divine life? What might it mean for daily Christian practice?

4. *Ordinary to Sacred Space:* The concept of a stable becoming a sanctuary appears in both the original meditation and the prayer. How do you see ordinary spaces being changed into sacred ones in your own experience?

5. *Christmas Characters:* The prayer mentions different witnesses to Christ's birth—Mary, shepherds, and angels—each with distinct roles. Which of these figures do you most identify with in your own faith journey, and why?

6. *Metaphors Matter:* How does the image of a "circle of love" and "dance" shape your understanding of God's relationship with humanity differently than more hierarchical images might?

7. *Making Moments:* The prayer speaks of "every moment holds Your presence." How might this perspective change how we think about sacred time versus ordinary time, especially beyond the Christmas season?

8. *In Need of a Blessing:* What aspects of our contemporary world do you see most in need of being "turned from curse to blessing?"

9. *Emmanuel:* The text explores the meaning of "Emmanuel" as both a name and a song/carol. How does thinking of God's presence as a kind of music or dance affect your understanding of divine-human relationship? What might it mean for non-human creation to participate in this divine dance? How does this inform our environmental responsibility?

CHRISTMAS EVE (NO INTERACTIVES)

CHRISTMAS DAY: THE ENCHANTMENT OF WONDER

Three devotions for Christmas Day designed to engage all generations present:

1. The Wonder of Gifts (Focus: Giving and Presence)

Read aloud the section of the meditation that focuses on giving and presence, starting with, "As we celebrate today, let each gift we share . . ." and ending with ". . . people forever changed by the simple, stunning truth that Love chose to dwell among us that first Christmas. And still does."

      Intergenerational Discussion:

- *Younger Children:* What's the best gift you ever received? Why? What's a gift you can give someone that doesn't cost money?
- *Older Children/Teens:* What does it mean to give your presence, not just presents? How can we show someone we are truly present with them?
- *Adults:* Reflecting on the past year, what's one way you felt the "presence" of someone in your life? How can we cultivate a spirit of presence in our families and communities?
- *Activity:* Have everyone write down (or draw, for younger children) one "gift of presence" they will give to someone in the coming year. This could be a promise to spend more time with them, help them with a task, or simply listen without interruption. These can be placed under the Christmas tree or in a special box to be revisited next Christmas.

- *Prayer:* A simple prayer of thanks for the gift of Jesus and for the ability to give and receive love.

2. The Wonder of the Manger (Focus: Humility and Simplicity)

Read aloud the section of the meditation that begins, "The Greatest Gift arrived not in gilded paper . . ." and ends with ". . . find magic in acts of ordinary kindness, to recognize holiness in human hearts."

Intergenerational Discussion:

- *Younger Children:* Why was Jesus born in a stable? What does a manger look like? Why is it important to be humble?
- *Older Children/Teens:* How does the story of Jesus' birth challenge our ideas about what is important or valuable? How can we find "magic in acts of ordinary kindness"?
- *Adults:* How can we simplify our lives to focus on what truly matters? How can we cultivate a spirit of humility in our families?
- *Activity:* If possible, create from scratch or mix-and-match from what's already there a simple manger scene together. Even just using a box and some fabric can be a meaningful activity. Talk about the symbolism of each element as you create it.
- *Prayer:* A prayer focusing on gratitude for the simple gifts in our lives and asking for help to see the sacred in the ordinary.

3. The Wonder of Wounds (Focus: Healing and Redemption)

Read the section that begins, "The wonder deepens when we

recognize . . ." and ends with ". . . mystery blossoms into the dawn's brightest star."

Intergenerational Discussion

- *Younger Children:* (Focus on the idea of healing) When you get a boo-boo, what helps you feel better? Jesus helps us feel better inside when we are sad or hurt.
- *Older Children/Teens:* What are some things that can "wound" us emotionally or spiritually? How can difficult experiences lead to growth and healing?
- *Adults:* How have you experienced healing or redemption in your own life? How can we offer support and healing to others who are hurting?
- *Activity:* Have everyone write down (or draw) something they are struggling with or a "wound" they are carrying. Then, write down a prayer or intention for healing and place it in a designated space. This symbolizes releasing those burdens and seeking healing.
- *Prayer:* A prayer acknowledging our brokenness and asking for God's healing touch, as well as the strength to be a source of healing for others.

HOGMANAY INTERACTIVES

1. *Cultivating Kindness:* How can the spirit of "first-footing," with its emphasis on welcoming both friends and strangers, inspire us to cultivate greater kindness and connection in our daily lives, particularly when it comes to those who are different from us or with whom we have had disagreements? What are some tangible ways we might "first-foot" and "share cups of kindness" with both friends and strangers in the coming year? What makes it particularly challenging to extend kindness to strangers?

2. *Prayer Posture:* The text contrasts the "bum kneel" with the "orant" posture of prayer. Which prayer posture resonates more with your faith journey right now, and why? How does our physical posture in prayer reflect or influence our inner state of being?

3. *Answered Prayers:* The meditation suggests that we are not just people who pray, but are ourselves "answers to prayer." How does this perspective shift your understanding of your place in God's work? Can you share a time when you realized you might have been an answer to someone else's prayer?

4. *Authentic Prayer:* The text explores Jesus' approach to prayer length, suggesting he valued "sincerity over showmanship, quality over quantity, heart attitude over formal structure." How do you balance these elements in your own prayer life? What helps you maintain authenticity in prayer?

5. *Praying the Bible:* "The Bible is not meant to be read. The Bible is meant to be prayed. You pray it as you read it and you read it as you pray it." How does this quote from Douglas Small strike you? What if you resolved to "pray" the Bible this year more than "read" the Bible?

6. *Navigating Tradition:* There's a recurring theme of old and new coexisting—ancient practices meeting present moments. How do you navigate between honoring traditional faith practices while making them relevant for today? What traditional practices have you found particularly meaningful?

7. *Continued Story:* The text suggests that we are "not beginning something new, but continuing an ancient story." How does this perspective affect how you think about your New Year's resolutions or intentions? How might it change your approach to growth as a Jesus human?

8. *Cherished Relationships:* The meditation describes divine mysteries "not as principles to master but as relationships to cherish." How does this distinction challenge or affirm your approach to discipleship. What might change if we approached our faith more as relationship than as mastery?

9. *From Head to Heart:* The closing prayer speaks of letting "doctrine become devotion and theology become testimony." Can you share an example from your own life where head knowledge turned into heart experience? What facilitated that transfiguration?

Notes

DEDICATION MEDITATION: THE HUMBLE BEARER

1. Laura Hobgood-Oster, *Holy Dogs and Asses: Animals in the Christian Tradition*, p. 69: "Stories of the Nativity of Jesus". These stories include images of adoring animals surrounding the manger. Cattle, sheep, donkeys, and the occasional dog or horse prove uncanny in their ability to recognize the revelation of the incarnation of the nativity . . . Images carved in marble, ivory, and stone from the earliest generations of Christianity show the donkey and the cow nuzzling the baby Jesus. In one of these, the donkey is obviously kissing him.

INTRODUCTION

1. Jon Meacham, *The Hope of Glory: Reflections on the Last Words of Jesus from the Cross* (2020), 41.

WEEK ONE

1. For more on a theology of "withness," see my book *11: Indispensable Relationship You Can't Live Without*, (2012).

WEEK THREE

1. Someone needs to write story of Jesus' life from the perspective of his silences, as seen in this Pilate interrogation (Matthew 27:14).
2. *The Tablet*, 09 June 2018.
3. Steven Chase, *The Tree of Life: Models of Christian Prayer* (2005), 10.

CHRISTMAS EVE

1. Sonnet LXII

CHRISTMAS DAY

1. Composer: George J. Elvey (1868), Public Domain.

HOGMANAY—NEW YEAR BEGINNING

1. Hogmanay is the Scots word for the last day of the old year and is synonymous with the celebration of the New Year in the Scottish manner.

INTERACTIVES

1. Kofi Annan was a Ghanaian diplomat who served as the seventh Secretary-General of the United Nations from 1997 to 2006. Annan and the UN were jointly awarded the Nobel Peace Prize in 2001. His long-time secretary ("Jacob") personally told me at the Maramon Convention in India that one morning they found two pipe bombs ready to explode in the meditation room and break the silence, which is what prompted the UN to install metal detectors.

About the Author

Websites:

leonardsweet.com

preachthestory.com

sanctuaryseaside.com

Podcasts:

Leonardsweet.com/podcasts

Napkin Scribbles Podcast (Spotify & Itunes)

instagram.com/leonard.sweet

facebook.com/lensweet

x.com/lensweet

youtube.com/leonardsweet1

www.ingramcontent.com/pod-product-compliance
Lightning Source LLC
Chambersburg PA
CBHW030557080526
44585CB00012B/401